*The Delights of
a Rare Book Librarian*

The Delights of
a Rare Book Librarian

by FREDERICK R. GOFF

Delivered on the occasion of the

second annual Bromsen Lecture

April 27, 1974

BOSTON

Trustees of the Public Library of the City of Boston

1975

Maury A. Bromsen Lecture
in Humanistic Bibliography, No. 2

Library of Congress Cataloging in Publication Data

Goff, Frederick Richmond, 1916–
    The delights of a rare book librarian.

    (Maury A. Bromsen lecture in humanistic bibliography; no. 2)
    Includes bibliographical references.
    1. Bibliography—Rare books—Addresses, essays, lectures.
I. Title.   II. Series.
Z1029.G62   016.09   75-4706
ISBN 0-89073-001-6

Foreword

The Boston Public Library is pleased to present in book form the second annual Maury A. Bromsen Lecture in Humanistic Bibliography. Mr. Bromsen, bookman and scholar in the field of bibliography and the history of the Americas, has endowed this lectureship in memory of his mother, Rose Eisenberg Bromsen (1885–1968). It is stipulated that "the speaker ought to emphasize the humanistic rather than the descriptive character of his subject. The lecture should be substantively historical and relate to printed material and its relationship to the evolution of thought."

In "The Delights of a Rare Book Librarian" Dr. Frederick R. Goff, whose name has long been synonymous with rare books in the United States, shares with his readers their common humanism. The world of rare books, remote and highly specialized as it might seem to the lay person, nevertheless stimulates appreciative reactions whether in response to the beauty of old texts; to historical associations like the earliest map identifying one area as America; or to the wonder at the continuity of human knowledge and experience that the rare book presents for consolation as well as joy.

v

Dr. Goff served for many years as Chief of the Rare Book Division of the Library of Congress. During his tenure he guided the growth of the collections from 127,000 items to more than 300,000 books and pamphlets and over 27,000 broadsides. In this lecture he sets forth a warm and civilized view of the painstaking research, the honest evaluations, the areas of competition, the detective story techniques, and the genuine excitement of discovery and competition. We are pleased to add this publication to the many scholarly contributions of Dr. Goff.

PHILIP J. McNIFF
DIRECTOR

The Delights of a Rare Book Librarian

RARE BOOK LIBRARIANS are a happy breed of men and women. We share common experiences and common pleasures, but there is nothing common about us. There is excitement in our lives for we work daily with the fabric of what has made the world what it is. We are an integral part of that world. We are frightfully competitive but almost never vicious or unkind to one another. At least that has been my experience during the nearly forty years that I have been privileged to be a member of this great fraternity. There are no saints among us that I know of, but we are blessed in many ways. As temporary custodians of the world's greatest books and manuscripts which record man's highest and also his lowest aspirations and his unending struggle to understand the world about him, to improve or to change it, or even unwittingly to destroy it, we share a personal destiny with the world of the past and the expectations and hope of the world to come. We are concerned. We have a sense of humor. We are aware that we have a special privilege to understand the motivations of a special mystique. Perhaps Thomas Carlyle expressed it better than anyone when he wrote (if I may paraphrase) that all that mankind has ever said or done is preserved as if by magic in the printed pages of books.

We may not write any great new pages ourselves in this record, but we are peculiarly sensitive to our surroundings for these books speak to us daily as we make our rounds. They are friends, and we realize how much we can learn from them, not only from their authors and their texts, but from the men who printed and published these texts, their binders, those who owned them, and those who collected them. The rare book librarian derives delight from such surroundings, and he responds in different ways to learn the secrets of his wares as they reveal their hidden and even majestic qualities, and to share the stories and the history that they quietly unfold at his bidding.

The delights of the rare book librarian are many, but no one to my knowledge has precisely defined just what it is that attracts one to these special friends. But we do know the pleasures they engender as we endeavor to unravel the secrets they contain, and to enjoy the excitement they create not only for us, but for the scholar, the collector, the bibliographer, and last but not least the bookseller. It is an interesting quintet, but the interchange that goes on among us is a compelling element which binds us one to the other. In my talk this evening I intend to be selfish and will address myself to some of the personal delights I have enjoyed as a bibliophile, as an acquisitor, as a bibliographer, but not I trust as a fool.

One of the delights in pursuing research according to "The Bibliographical Way"—a phrase used as the title of one of Lawrence Wroth's essays—is the satisfaction of relating one book to another through the coincidence of provenance. A recent acquisition of the Rare Book Division of the Library of Congress provides an excellent example of this kind of coincidence. Late in October of 1967 the third portion of the

Documents for a system of education in Virginia.
Letters &c. on University education.
Rules & statutes of the University of Pensylva.
Boyle on Orthography.
Duponceau's English Phonology
Connecticut asylum of deaf & dumb.
Ware's new principles of education.
Fellenberg sur les instituts d'Education à Hofwyl
Jullien sur l'education comparée
Instruction primaire.
Principes generaux sur l'instruction par le Marquis de B.
Rapports sur l'Instruction elementaire.

Thomas Jefferson's handwriting

1. List of pamphlets on education in Thomas Jefferson's handwriting, bound into a single volume.

Americana library of the late Thomas W. Streeter was sold at auction in New York. Included in the sale was a volume of twelve pamphlets with the leather label on the spine reading "Pamphlets Education," and a list of the pamphlets in Jefferson's handwriting on the fly-leaf (Figure 1). I am happy that the Library of Congress was the successful bidder. This has especial pertinence for the collections housed within the national library for a number of reasons. More than any other single person Mr. Jefferson can be regarded as the true founder of the Library of Congress in those early days of its inception back in the first decade of the 19th century. Later when the original Library of Congress was reduced to ashes during the evening of August 24, 1814, it was President Jefferson's library that served as the phoenix. His personal library remains today as the nucleus around which the Library has developed to its present position of eminence. After Jefferson "ceded" his library to Congress in 1815—his polite way of describing the financial details of its sale—he formed another library during the remaining eleven years of his lifetime, and this pamphlet volume on education was a part of this second library which, while destined for the University of Virginia, was sold for compelling reasons of financial necessity in the city of Washington on the 27th of February in 1829.

It is a well-known fact that in designing his own tombstone, Thomas Jefferson specified that he wished to be remembered for three specific things: "Author of the Declaration of American Independence, of the Statute of Virginia for religious freedom, & Father of the University of Virginia." Not one more word was to be added to the obelisk he designed to mark his grave, for by these, he wrote, "as testimonials that I have lived, I wish most to be remembered." And it is the last of this trio, his founding of the University of Virginia, which concerns us here, for the first pamphlet in the volume is entitled "Sundry Documents on the Subject of a System of Public Education for the State of Virginia" (Richmond, 1817). This pamphlet includes Jefferson's "Bill for the more general diffusion of Knowledge," which was largely rejected by the State Assembly. A letter from him explaining his plan for schools in Virginia including "the Academy or College proposed to be established in our neighborhood," that is, in Albemarle County, is also printed in the pamphlet. The final section is a "Report of the President and Directors of the Literary Fund, to the General Assembly, in December 1816," which includes a proposal concerning "the establishment of an University, to be called '*The University of Virginia.*' "

Other pamphlets and articles in the volume are concerned with principles of education, university education, and orthography and phonology. He was seriously interested in orthography and advocated simplified spelling that was representative of pronunciation. In 1815 he even commented on the "favorable tho' slow progression in our orthography, altho' the dictionary makers have not ventured to admit it." In addition to reflecting Thomas Jefferson's interest and activity in education, the contents of this volume are valuable as documents in educational philosophy at a time when popular education was just developing.

The volume at one time was in the library of Jefferson's granddaughter's husband, Nicholas P. Trist, and contains his bookplate. He may have bought the book at the sale of Jefferson's library held in Washington on February 27, 1829. At any rate it now reposes, after a few minor repairs, in a new slipcase next to a similar volume of pamphlets on the same subject which was sold as lot 226 at that auction. In Jefferson's own manuscript catalogue this volume was entered as number 227, and the one recently acquired was number 212. After a separation of 145 years these two volumes are now placed side by side in almost their original relationship to one another.

Another instance of reassemblage of related volumes through a common provenance takes us back first to the 18th century and thence to the later years of the 15th century. In 1930 the Library of Congress acquired the Vollbehr Collection of 3,000 incunabula by an Act of Congress at the price of one and a half million dollars. Included among them were thirty-nine 15th-century books that formerly were in the library of the Benedictine monastery of St. Peter's at Salzburg (Figure 2). These were scattered among the other books in

2. Incunabula formerly in St. Peter's monastery at Salzburg with their characteristic white leather backs, now in the Library of Congress.

the collection, but they were quite readily recognizable since their backs or spines were covered in the middle of the 18th century with a white sheepskin or pigskin onlay and new identifying leather labels, or else they were entirely rebound in white pigskin in the style of many German bindings of the 16th century. The purpose was purely one of interior decoration. The Abbot of the monastery or his librarian decided during an extensive renovation of the abbey to change this monastery's library into a "white" library, which was the vogue in Austria at that time. The extensive sampling from the original library suggests the baroque elegance that the renovated library at St. Peter's must have presented to the observer.

The books rising on the shelves were very much a part of the architectural presentation, and the expedient of covering the original backs with white sheepskin and adding new leather labels with gold lettering must have achieved a stunning effect. Other "white" libraries apparently were more economically achieved through the application of a coat of white paint to the spines of earlier bindings. Only one such example is found in the Library of Congress group, and the paint has become gray with age. Very likely this volume was added after the extensive refurbishing was completed, and the expediency of a little white paint solved the problem of adding to the shelves an otherwise discordant volume.

In the group of volumes under discussion no less than twenty-three appear to have been bound in the same bindery for each shares in common at least one and usually several of the stamps and rolls that are identical. This bindery used a wide variety of tools and rolls, some sixty in number. One or more were frequently used together to form interesting variations in design.

The most outstanding example of a binding from this bindery, which we localize at Salzburg and most probably within

St. Peter's monastery itself, is found on a German Bible printed at Nuremberg between 1476 and 1478. When Miss Dorothy Miner of the Walters Art Gallery in Baltimore was assembling material for the history-making exhibition of bindings, held in that city from November 1957 to January 1958, she selected these two volumes for inclusion. They figure as entries 157 and 158 in the published catalogue, *The History of Bookbinding 525–1950 A.D.* The bindings are wooden boards covered with reddish brown goatskin. The front or upper cover of volume one is decorated in the form of a saltire impressed repeatedly with a tool of a branch wound with a scroll lettered O MARAI (for O MARIA). The four triangles created by the saltire are decorated with the oak-leaf pattern produced by the cusped edging tool and veining; in the center of each there is a rosette. The outer frame surrounding the central design is composed of square rosettes with circular ones in each of the four corners. The lower cover is diapered into a number of lozenges each filled with the oak-leaf design produced with a smaller edging tool than was used on the upper cover. On the spine the lettered scroll is repeated as well as the small edging tool and a shield with a flowering potted plant. The upper cover of the second volume presents a rectangular border with an inner field divided by a saltire stamped with rows of "free" roses which also appear in the four corners. In the outer border twin tendrils in the form of a Gothic arch, known to binders as a crocketed ogive tool, have produced lozenges, containing a flower of six petals with tendrils to which a strawberry is affixed, all within a diamond. This tool also appears in the center of the saltire and on the panel of the spine. Another stamp, a circular tool with an orchid-like flower, is used four times in the inner field. It is interesting to note that all four covers and both spines are stamped differently, which seems to have been the common practice of this bindery. The white sheepskin coverings which probably had been added to the spines have now been removed.

Miss Miner also selected for inclusion in the Baltimore exhibit another 15th-century book from the Library of Congress. From internal evidence it is apparent that this binding was executed for the monastery of St. Peter and St. Paul located at Erfurt, in Southern Germany. The further study of this blind-stamped binding led to some interesting disclosures which we published in an article prepared for the 1969 *Gutenberg-Jahrbuch*. The text of the volume itself comprises a collection of Lenten sermons of Johannes Gritsch, which Anton Koberger, who incidentally was the godfather of Albrecht Dürer, printed at Nuremberg in 1481. In the description of this brown pigskin binding in the Baltimore catalogue, Miss Miner refers to several of the stamps, notably a large circular rose, a circular Agnus Dei, a small circular pelican in its piety, a pointed oval of a fleur-de-lys with two perching birds, a small square eagle displayed, and what she describes as a "very unusual square stamp of a nude figure seated and holding up a wreath—suggestive in design of an antique gem." Several years ago we recognized this same stamp an l several others used on this binding on another binding, this one of stout white pigskin over wooden boards. The gem-like stamp is used repeatedly in the central panel and in the borders at the top and bottom. This volume—a miscellaneous assemblage of diverse manuscripts—also was bound for the monastery of St. Peter and St. Paul in Erfurt. The remaining parts of the clasp affixed to the top cover appear to be identical to those found on the binding of the Gutenberg Bible that was executed at Erfurt by Johann Fogel and which now reposes on the shelves of the library at Eton College. What connection Fogel may have had with the binders operating within the monastery of St. Peter and St. Paul is unknown, but at least they appear to have used the same supplier inso-

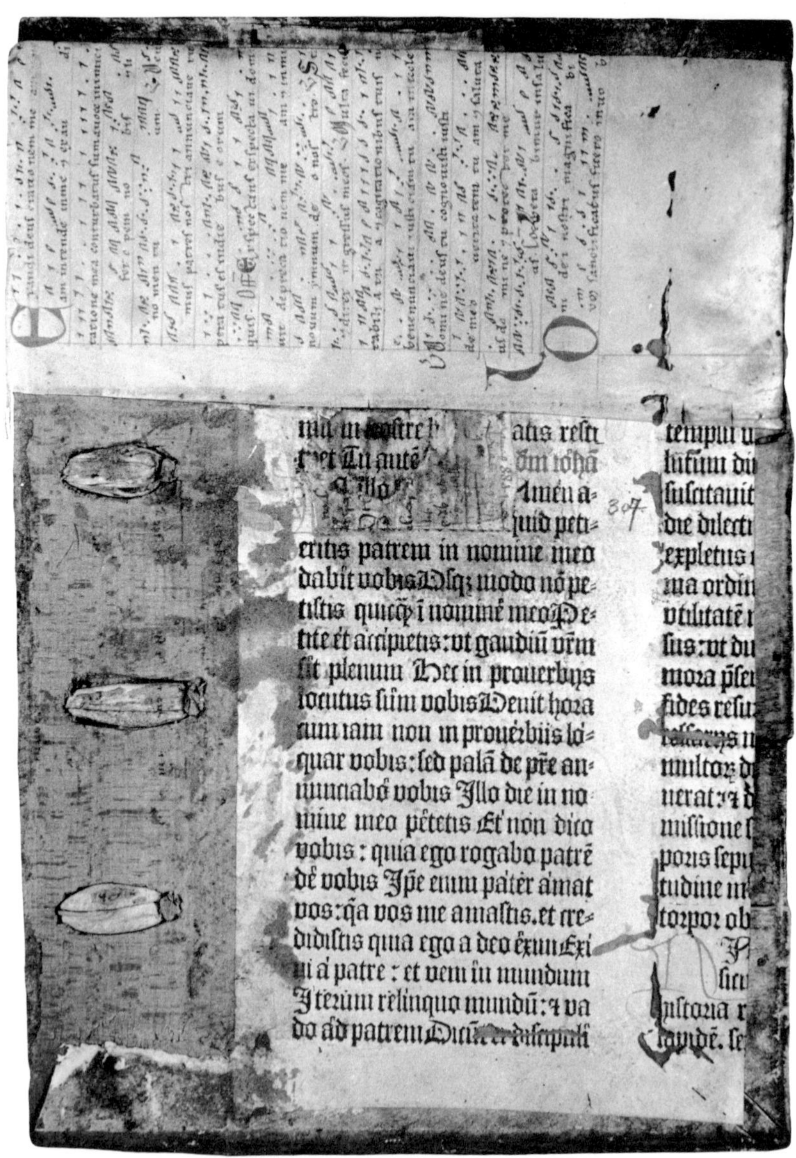

3. Lining paper of the back cover of Petrus de Palude's
Sermones thesauri novi de sanctis (Strassburg, 1484).

far as these brass clasps are concerned. A third binding with many of the identical stamps, but not in as fresh a condition, is found on the Library's copy of Petrus de Palude's *Sermones thesauri novi de sanctis*, printed at Strassburg in 1484 (*Third Census* P-509). The first leaf bearing the title is wanting, and there is now no indication in the text of the volume that this belonged originally to the same monastery. The certainty of this provenance, however, is proved by one of the lining papers of the back cover (Figure 3). This proves to be a partial leaf of one and one-quarter columns from the rare *Lectionarium*, printed at the monastery and dated December 24, 1479; it is regarded as the first known book to be printed in Erfurt. No copy of the complete work is available in this country, nor is there a copy in the British Museum.

How this was identified is a rather involved story which need not be explained here, but a similar example where two leaves of printer's waste were used as lining leaves will serve to describe the process more concretely. The examples in mind are taken from the inside back cover of a copy of Petrus Berchorius' *Liber Bibliae moralis*, printed at Ulm by Johann Zainer in 1474 (Figure 4). At first glance these appear to be two conjugate leaves from an unidentified book of sermons. After spending a little time studying these leaves, they have been identified as belonging to an edition of Guilelmus Parisiensis' *Postilla*, printed at Augsburg by Johann Wiener in 1475, of which, incidentally, we can locate only the one copy in Munich. How was this identification possible? It is principally due to the pioneer work of a distinguished German incunabilist—Dr. Konrad Haebler. Nearly seventy years ago he published one of his best-known works, the *Typenrepertorium der Wiegendrucke*. In his analysis of Gothic types, to which our specimen belongs, he identified 101 different forms of the capital letter M. The capital M in the leaves shown belongs to Haebler's number 13. Haebler's systematic analysis of

Gothic types, arranged according to the M-form, is based upon the millimeter measurement of twenty lines of type—in this instance 113 mm.

Consulting Haebler's tables, one finds that no such type of this dimension is listed. In surveying similar types, however, it is evident that a number of printers at Augsburg or the neighboring towns used this particular capital M. We next consulted Konrad Burger's *Monumenta Germaniae et Italiae typographia* and found the type we were looking for reproduced on table 53. Why we failed to find this type recorded in Haebler is explained by the fact that when first cast twenty lines of this type measured 120 mm., and this is how Haebler records it. Later it was recast on a smaller body with a reduced measurement of 113 mm. for twenty lines of type. Burger's facsimile is taken from the Munich copy of the 1475 edition of the *Postilla* of Guilelmus Parisiensis, which, if not unique, is indeed a rare book. The Library's conjugate leaf is also taken from this first dated edition of one of the best-sellers of the 15th century.

Let us now consider other kinds of evidence that can assist the bibliographer in localizing unsigned or fragmentary pieces of early printing. A few years ago Mr. Lessing Rosenwald acquired for his print collection, now an integral part of the National Gallery of Art, an interesting broadside of a poem written by Jacob Locher, the German poet laureate, in praise of King Maximilian (Figure 5). The poem takes for its text the first chapter in Ezechiel wherein the prophet sees four living creatures, each with four faces, one human, and the others those of lions, oxen, and eagles. Locher relates these to the Evangelists. The printer presumably decided to use five appropriate woodcuts that he had available in his stock, and he arranged them as a unit at the top. There is no statement present on the sheet to indicate the place of printing, the printer, or the date. Using the woodcuts as a clue,

4. Lining paper of the back cover of Petrus Berchorius' *Liber Bibliae moralis* (Ulm, 1474).

Carmē Jacobi locher philomusi poete laureati In faciē Aquile ⁊ laudē inuictissimi Maximiliani Romanoꝛ regis

Hec facies Aquile mysteria certa figurat
  Vt referunt legis dogmata scripta noue.
Quatuor Ezechiel facies vidisse propheta
  Dicitur: et pariter plurime fata dei.
Matheus Vna fuit faciés hominis: quā rite Matheus
  Ostendit: quiddam Religionis habet:
Humanos quoniam Christi narrauerit actus
  Naturamꝗ hominis: Imperiumꝗ dei:
Marcus In facie Marcus rigidi: formaꝗ leonis
  Pingitur:Illud emin non racione vacat.
Nam regnū Christi firmū. Sceptrūꝗ figurat:
  Qui rex est regum maximus:est ꝗ deus.
Lucas Et bouis in facie lucas formatus: Idipsum
  Significat.quod nūc carmia nostra probent
Nam bos est animal aptum feruentibus aris
  Sacrorum: dignum Thuricremisꝗ focis.
Per quod signantur christi custodia templi:
  Atꝗ sacerdotij prestita iurra sui:
Iohannes Sed quia nūc facies Aquile volitantis ad axes
  Aethereos: Sancti corda iohannis habet
In christo nostro naturam: credite: signat
  Diuinam: ad celos altius ipse volat
Verbi incarnati mysteria celica scribit
  Et reserat celos: Astriferosꝗ choros.
Non in terrenis solum vestigia rebus
  Ponit: At insigni sydera fronte ferit:
Sunt alie cause: mira ratione: probate:
  Cur facies aquile dignior vsꝗ fiet.
Nā tribus exuperans aliorum scripta iohannes
  Insignem vultum continet ipse sibi.
Omnibus en scripsit per fectius: eximiusꝗ.
  Subtilesꝗ magis transiit ille vias.

Atꝗ oculos fixit celeres adcelica castra
  Lustrauitꝗ deum. Celicolasꝗ choros.
Non igitur frustra romani dextera regis
  Victrices aquilas gestat: et ore fouet.
Nam gratus superis nō hec terrena gubernat
  Tantum: sed mentem vertit ad astra poli:
Contemplatur eni quo nūc a numine sceptrū
  Ceperit ipse: suum.fasti gerum ꝗ decus.
Et gestat meritis Aquilam Cōpluribus auctus
  Imperio solus dignus ad esse potest:
Excellitꝗ alios triplici: Rex: munere regis
  Et dominos: terre.Magnanimosꝗ duces.
Excellit regno tarpeio quod deus olim
  Constituit: fines et. sine fine dedit:
Excellit signis Aquile rutilaꝗ corona
  Et gladio: mundi quo scelera ipsa premit
Cultibus excellit diuinis: legibus atꝗ
  Rex sacrosanctis. Relligione quoꝗ:
Hunc precor ad nutū defendas sancte iohānes
  Qui portat vultus celica signa tui.
Fac precor vt celsas restauret Cesaris Arces:
  Augeat et Regni limina vasta sui:
Sis precor Auxilio Regi: tua numina mitte:
  Interras: Aquilam dilige queso tuam:
Rex quia Romane tentat componere sedem
  Ecclesie: Sacras et reparare domos.
In Thurcos rapidos bellantia signa reducet.
  Prosternet Persas classibus atꝗ feros.
Excutiet falsos cultores atꝗ propheras.
  Vrbibus a sacris: purget et omne nefas:
Da precor Auxilium.Regē defende benignū
  Sic mihi proueniant vota petita velim.

5. Broadside of a poem by Jacob Locher in praise of King Maximilian.

6. Title page of the *Evangelia* (Strassburg, 1498).

however, we consulted Albert Schramm's monumental twenty-three volume work, which, while remaining incomplete, attempted to reproduce all of the woodcuts used as illustrations in German incunabula. The woodcuts we were seeking are located in figure 466 on plate 67 (Figure 6), in volume XX.

15

Schramm reproduces them as they appear on the title page of an edition of the *Evangelia*, which was first printed at Strassburg by Johann Grüninger in 1498 and later in 1500. They were obviously prepared to accompany this text since they represent the four Evangelists with St. John in the center and with the young Christ Child in the upper left-hand corner. After making typographical comparisons it may be stated without hesitation that in all probability the Rosenwald broadside was also printed at Strassburg by Johann Grüninger about 1500.

Not only woodcuts but even simple initials can sometimes prove invaluable in assigning a book to a given place and printer. A few years ago the Library purchased for its Rosenwald Collection a fine copy of Henry VIII's *Assertio septem sacramentorum adversus Martin. Lutherum*, printed at London in 1521. This book has excited me ever since I handled one of the copies printed on vellum which is now in the Vatican Library. This was the very same copy that Henry VIII himself had presented to the then Pope, Leo X. In return for this defence of the Papacy against Luther, he received the title of "Defender of the Faith"—a title which the English monarch carries to this day. This important book, in which King Henry made an absolute admission of Papal authority, had one of the "most fateful impacts upon Western civilization of any printed book" since it "must be considered a cardinal, if not a motive, force in the history of the English Reformation." The acquisition of the first edition of 1521 led to an examination of other later editions in the Library's collection. One of these, without any clue to its place of origin on the title page and without a colophon, had been assigned to Paris and dated about 1522, on the basis of a manuscript note on the title page of another copy of this edition in the British Museum. In our examination of the book, we noticed an attractive initial Q (Figure 7). After considerable searching

INDVLGEN

TIAE SVNT ADVLATORVM
ROMANORVM NEQVITIAE.

VEMAD=
modum animal
omne potißimu
ex facie dinoſca=
tur, ita ex hac
quoq; prima.P=
poſitione clare=
ſcat, quã ſuppu=
ratum ac putri=
dum is habeat
cor, cuius os ama

ritudine plenum, tali exundat ſanie. Nã quæ de indul=
gentijs olim diſſeruit, ea plærisq;, multum uidebantur
adimere non modo de poteſtate pontificis, uerumetiã de
bona ſpe ac ſancta conſolatione fidelium, hominesq; ue=
hementer animare, ut in pœnitentiæ ſuæ cõfiſi diuitijs,
eccleſiæ theſaurum & ultroneam dei benignitatem cõ
temnerent. Et tamen ea quæ tum ſcripſit omnia, idcirco
mitius accepta ſunt, quia plæraq; diſſerebat dumtaxat,
non aſſerebat. Subinde etiam petens doceri, ſeſeq; polli=
cens meliora docenti pariturum. Verum iſtud quã ſim=   Lutheri fi=
                                                                         ctio.

A 5   pliciæ ſcri=

7. Initial Q used by Johann Schoeffer at Mainz.

this identical initial was noticed in Alfred F. Johnson's *Decorative Initial Letters* (London, 1931). He identifies these initials as having been used by Johann Schoeffer at Mainz in his edition of Livy which appeared in 1518. Johnson tells us that Schoeffer's books of the Reformation, like those of his contemporaries, are lavishly decorated with woodcuts, or metalcuts, borders, initials, and illustrations. The name of the artist who designed them is not known, but the initials with figures clearly show the influence of Hans Holbein. The woodcut border surrounding the title and the italic type used throughout corroborate the attribution to Johann Schoeffer at Mainz about 1522, which is about as valid an imprint as one can establish.

In this presentation thus far we have been concerned with positive evidence possessed by certain books which has been utilized in their specific identification and localization. The bibliographer and bibliophile must also be aware of how certain books have been doctored or tampered with. A good illustration is furnished by William Caxton's edition of Jacobus de Voragine's *Golden Legend*, a compendium of the lives of the saints, printed at Westminster about 1483. This is the most extensive of Caxton's works both in text and in illustrations. The most interesting parts of the text concern English saints whose lives do not appear in the Continental editions of this popular hagiography. One of the woodcuts depicts the murder of St. Thomas à Becket in Canterbury Cathedral. In one of the two copies in the Library of Congress this cut and the accompanying text is original and has not been altered in any way. In many of the surviving copies of this edition, including the one in the Boston Public Library, this leaf has been excised due to the suppression by Henry VIII of a Becket cult which we readily recognize today through references to the "Canterbury pilgrimage." In 1538 King Henry ordered Becket's shrine in Canterbury Cathedral destroyed.

here /   The reuerend fader in god /
Stephen Archebisshop of caunterburpe
Rychard bisshop of salisbury/ Waltere
the pryour of the same place wyth the
couent wyth spyrytual songe and de ,
uoute ymphes whan it was nyght
went to the sepulcre of this holy mar,
tir/ And alle that nyght/ and day of
                                        B iiij

8. Pen-and-ink facsimile by John Harris, Jr., which replaces a missing page in Jacobus de Voragine's *Golden Legend*.

Later that year he issued a proclamation declaring that the death of Thomas was "untruly called martydom" and henceforth he was no longer to be called St. Thomas of Canterbury, but Bishop Becket; all images and pictures were to be put down, and his name was to be erased from the calendar and all service books. The page in one of the copies in Washington escaped mutilation, which was not the case with its counterpart in another copy of the 1483 edition, now a part of the Library of Congress' distinguished Rosenwald Collection. A pen-and-ink facsimile very carefully executed by John Harris, Jr., has been substituted; this is one of several such facsimile pages he executed to perfect the text of this copy. One should make it clear that this is an honest facsimile, not a forgery. In fact the talented artist who executed the facsimile leaf has very carefully added his initials "J. H. jun" in miniscule letters just above the last line of the text (Figure 8), as the blown-up reproduction readily reveals. As an artisan with this special talent Harris (and his father as well) were very much in demand, and a wealthy generation of English book collectors kept them actively employed for just such purposes as this one.

Other less honest facsimiles have plagued the book collector and the bibliographer, not to mention the bookseller, for as long as rare and valuable books have been esteemed and collected there have been scoundrels who have doctored many imperfect copies to make them more saleable at higher prices than their condition warranted.

A deliberate instance of forgery is evidenced through a doctored colophon found in a copy of Giovanni Boccaccio's *Il Decamerone*. In 1951 we exchanged correspondence with the late Frank Glenn, a bookseller of Kansas City, concerning what he believed was an unrecorded edition of an early edition of *Il Decamerone*, printed at Venice by the brothers De Gregorii, and dated June 20 in 1492. In the various published sources devoted to the career of the two brothers Giovanni and Gregorio, there was no record of such an edition. While an unusual situation this is not unheard of in this early period of printing, especially concerning popular books, many of which exist today in unique copies. The dealer arranged to send the volume for examination, and upon its arrival and after a careful perusal we concluded that the book appeared to be Venetian all right, but later in date than the colophon indicated. Now it so happened that the Library's Rosenwald Collection possesses a copy of a Venetian edition of *Il Decamerone*, printed by Augustus de Zanni in 1518. A comparison between the two originals confirmed our suspicion that the 1492 colophon was a forgery. The forger had taken an imperfect copy of the 1518 edition, lacking the final seven leaves, and erased from the explicit found on the leaf numbered CXIII the phrase: "Sequitan tre novelle nuouamete ritrouate." In its stead he added in matching types the names of the two

DeGregorii brothers as printers, and the date June 20, 1492. The original volume with the forged colophon was returned to Mr. Glenn; he subsequently died, and we do not know the present location of the forged copy. When last we talked with Mrs. Glenn, who continues to operate her husband's shop, she could furnish no clue to its present whereabouts. It was not reported for inclusion in the Third Census of *Incunabula in American Libraries*, so if this copy should be offered for sale, I trust the buyer will be forewarned.

Two years after the Boccaccio was printed, there appeared also at Venice an edition of Johannes Solinus' *Polyhistor* or, in its English title, *Marvels of the World*. It contains as a frontispiece a world map by Peter Apian that is dated 1520. Until the relatively recent discovery of a somewhat similar world map of Martin Waldseemüller dated 1507, this Apian map was regarded as the earliest one on which the name America

9. World map of 1530 inserted in the Library of Congress' copy of Pomponius Mela's *De orbis situ* (Basel, 1522).

appeared. This is found on the land mass corresponding to-day to the north and east coast of South America, beneath a text which reads in translation: "In the year 1497 this land with the adjacent islands was discovered by Columbus a Genoese under the mandate of the king of Castile."

Now in 1957 a dealer in Blaricum, the Netherlands, offered for sale a copy of Pomponius Mela's *De orbis situ*, in the edition published at Basel in 1522. As the work of the earliest Roman geographer, this is an interesting text, but what heightened my interest was a world map of 1530 (Figure 9) which had been inserted in it. It obviously did not belong to the text dated 1522, and when the volume arrived this fact was corroborated. It is evident that the map was inserted long after the book was published, since the wormholes in the leaves of text between which the map is inserted are in exact correspondence and the map itself shows no penetration by the worms. This "wormhole theory" of research, incidentally, has also been applied in testing the authenticity of the controversial Vinland map, but that need not concern us here. The 1530 world map also contains on the back traces of an adhesive suggesting that prior to its insertion in this volume it had probably been mounted in some fashion. But regardless of when it was done, we are profoundly grateful to whoever was responsible for saving it since it is one of the rarest of all of the early maps relating to America. At the time the dealer catalogued this copy he was not aware of this fact, for his cautious description suggested that there were five or six copies extant. There is no need to dwell on the details of the quest for descriptions of these other copies, but after a long correspondence we have concluded that only one other copy could be traced, and that has been owned by the John Carter Brown Library in Providence since 1846. Without wishing to appear to boast, it must be admitted that the present copy is superior in condition to the one in Providence, which lacks all four of the compass points, and a large tear in the upper right-hand corner seriously affects that portion of the map in the Pacific area south of Japan. There is no question that the engraver of this map, Peter de Wale of Antwerp, had a copy of Apian's map before him as he worked, but although a copy, it is a completely new engraving, and it is the earliest map engraved in Belgium to show America as the New World.

Another smaller and much later map (Figure 10) relates more directly to our area of the world. This is the Thackara and Vallance engraving of the city of Washington, which we have shown to be the earliest engraved map of the Federal City. The map reproduced is taken from a copy of Tobias Lear's *Observations on the River Potomack*, printed at New York in 1793. The map as well as the pamphlet are annotated by James Kent, who was later known as Chancellor Kent, a title he carried after his appointment to the New York Court of Chancery in 1814.

The "Plan of the City of Washington" was not intended to accompany the Lear pamphlet. Neither of the other two copies in the Library of Congress contains this plan, nor is it present in the two copies located by the National Union Catalog respectively at the Massachusetts Historical Society and the University of Virginia. It is evident, however, that the map accompanied the copy which Chancellor Kent annotated, since he has marked the map at seven places and identified them through a table of references.

The Thackara and Vallance plan which derives from Major L'Enfant's original drawing is of itself a map of considerable interest. While Pierre L'Enfant is responsible for the design of the Federal City, he experienced irreconcilable difficulties with the Commissioners. By September of 1793 his work in the Federal City terminated completely, although earlier, in 1792, he had been suspended. The Library of Con-

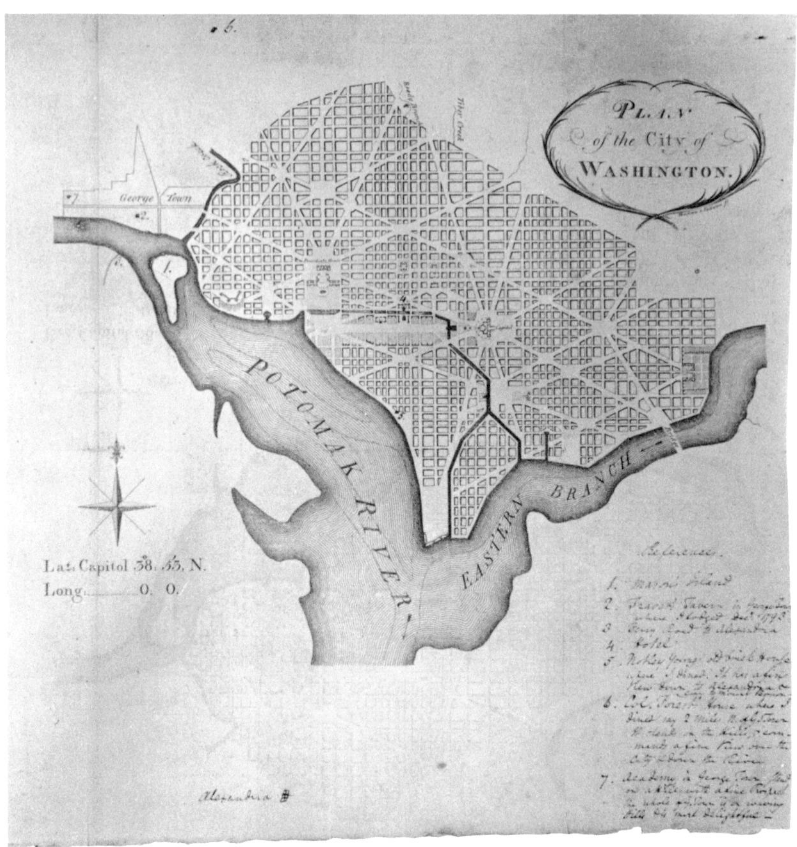

10. Thackara and Vallance's engraving of the city of Washington, inserted in Chancellor Kent's copy of Tobias Lear's *Observations on the River Potomack* (New York, 1793).

gress has L'Enfant's original manuscript map of Washington, which the designer is believed to have taken with him to Philadelphia for submission to President Washington on August 28, 1791. Somewhat later Andrew Ellicott, an assistant to L'Enfant and an early surveyor of the District of Columbia, went to Philadelphia for the purpose of preparing, with

24

the assistance of his brothers, a plan of the city of Washington, using as a basis a copy of L'Enfant's plan since L'Enfant himself apparently withheld his original plan. Mr. Ellicott wrote to the Commissioners about the situation on February 23, 1792, in these terms:

On my arrival at this City, I found that no preparation was made for an engraving of the plan of the City of Washington.—Upon this representation being made to the President and Secretary of State, I was directed to furnish one for an engraver; which with the aid of my Brother was compleated last monday, and handed to the President.—In this business we met with difficulties of a very serious nature.—Major L'Enfant refused us the use of the *Original*! What his motives were, God knows—The plan which we have furnished, I believe will be found to answer the ground better, than the large one in the Major's hands. I have engaged two good artists, (both americans,) to execute the engraving, and who will begin the work as soon, as the President comes to a determination respecting some small alterations.

The Ellicott plan was turned over both to Messrs. Thackara and Vallance, Philadelphia engravers, and to Samuel Blodget, Jr., who arranged for its engraving by Samuel Hill in Boston. Mr. Hill sent a proof sheet to Secretary of State Jefferson in Philadelphia, who wrote to the Commissioners on July 11, 1792:

I now send a proof sheet of the plan of the town engraving at Boston. I observe the soundings of the creek & river are not in it. It would be well to know of Mr. Ellicot whether they were in the original sent to Boston. if not, you will probably think it adviseable to insert them in this proof sheet, and send it to Boston, addressed to Mr. Blodget, under whose care the engraving is going on.

The next day Mr. Jefferson wrote to Mr. Blodget informing him of these facts. Apparently the recommendations did not reach Boston in time, for the Hill engraving does not contain the soundings. As a matter of fact, from correspondence exchanged between George Taylor, Jr., and Thomas Jefferson during August of 1792, we learn that the plate engraved by Samuel Hill was shipped to Philadelphia on the sloop *Juno* and arrived there on July 20. The steward at Jefferson's residence in Philadelphia laid it aside and Mr. Taylor did not receive it until August 16. On that date Taylor wrote to the Commissioners of his plans to have a Mr. Scott print the necessary edition of 4,000 copies. Since Mr. Scott was not able to begin printing for a week, he probably did not start until August 23, providing of course the Commissioners forwarded their approbation. Mr. Scott agreed to undertake the printing of about a hundred a day. At this rate the printing of the edition would not have been completed until early in October. We know from William Tindall's *Standard History of the City of Washington* (Knoxville, Tenn., 1914) that "the Boston Plate was completed in time to be exhibited at the second sale of lots on October 8, 1792."

Meanwhile Thackara and Vallance were preparing at Philadelphia their engraving of Ellicott's map, measuring 21 x 29 inches. This map is much larger than the Hill engraving (17 x 22 inches) and cost 4 shillings, 8½ pence, which was 2 shillings and 2½ pence more than the Hill engraving. The Thackara and Vallance plan of the city of Washington did not reach the Commissioners until November 13, according to Tindall. However, identical advertisements appeared in two Philadelphia newspapers, *Dunlap's American Daily Advertiser* and the *Gazette of the United States*, on September 15, 1792. This advertisement announced that "Plans of the City of Washington" are "to be sold by the booksellers, viz Dobson, Carey, Young and Crukshank." In the former newspaper it appeared at least four times during October and November and twice during December. This notice quite probably refers to both plans, not to the Philadelphia plan alone.

Several smaller engravings of Washington were made during 1792. Actually three of them were published before the larger engravings appeared. Messrs. Thackara and Vallance, apparently using Ellicott's plan as a prototype, engraved a plan measuring 8¼ x 10 inches (the plate is slightly larger). This appeared as the frontispiece in *The Universal Asylum, and Columbia Magazine* for March 1792, printed at Philadelphia "for the proprietors by William Young." The engravers' names appear beneath the wreath of the title.

This Thackara and Vallance small engraving based upon Ellicott's original plan is also used as the frontispiece added to Chancellor Kent's copy of Tobias Lear's *Observations*, dated 1793; it was again used as a frontispiece to the later edition of 1794. All of the foregoing information is probably presented in too much detail, but it seemed important to show that the frontispiece to the Lear pamphlet actually is a copy of the earliest engraved map of the city of Washington, first published in the March issue of *The Universal Asylum . . .* for 1792. As a matter of incidental information the paper on which it is engraved bears the watermark "S. L." (Samuel Loudon?).

Mr. Jefferson, as we all know, was a man of many parts. He figures as the founder of the University of Virginia at the commencement of this essay. It is certainly now evident that he was very much interested in the original maps of Washington. But his most enduring contribution to our country and to humanity at large is the immortal Declaration of Independence. We do not intend to discuss here his role in its composition or the bibliographical history of the printing of this great document, which my old friend Mike Walsh has handled so effectively in his definitive work on the contemporary broadside editions of the Declaration, acknowledging, of course, that no work of bibliography is ever definitive. I can add, however, a brief preamble of sorts. Mr. Walsh's study describes as entry number two the unique copy of the Declaration of Independence, printed on vellum, in the possession of the American Philosophical Society in Philadelphia. The imprint does not furnish the place of printing or the date, but it does state that it was printed by John Dunlap, who we know printed the text of the Declaration as adopted by the Continental Congress on the night of July 4, 1776.

Presumably the unique copy on vellum was printed by Dunlap at a somewhat later time, but someone must have realized that history was in the making and for reasons of preserving the text in more durable form arranged for this one copy to be printed on vellum. Some years ago we received an offer from a New England dealer of another and somewhat earlier example of John Dunlap's printing on vellum. Knowing of the latter's role in printing the vellum copy of the Declaration, and also being interested in the earliest printers' productions of vellum books, including one figure no less than Johann Gutenberg, I purchased for the Library of Congress what I believe to represent the earliest example of printing on vellum to have issued from an American press. This is a fragment of Rev. Jacob Duché's *Observations on a Variety of Subjects*. Occupying twenty-eight pages printed on twenty-eight leaves, the printed text, except for the first and final pages, is found on facing pages.

It is thus evident that Dunlap printed his text only on one side of the vellum sheet. The last page contains the following colophon: "PHILADELPHIA: / Printed by JOHN DUN-LAP; / IN MARKET-STREET / M,DCC,LXXIII." As far as we know this is a unique issue of Abbe Duché's first letter, printed one year before the larger work appeared in 1774. This fragment of twenty-eight leaves represents undoubtedly the earliest instance of an American book, even in abbreviated form, to be printed on vellum. Apparently it was prepared as a trial issue, or possibly Dunlap merely wished to experiment with printing on a difficult medium. The 1774 edition of Duché's book is fairly common, but it seems particularly significant that the text of the first letter on vellum contains interesting references to the State House (later Independence Hall), the Library Company of Philadelphia, the University of Pennsylvania, and Dr. Franklin.

At the time of acquisition in 1958 we also purchased what we then believed to be another unique example of printing—a broadside edition of Abraham Lincoln's *Gettysburg Address* captioned more precisely: "Oration of Abraham Lincoln at the Dedication of the Gettysburg National Military Cemetery, November 19, 1863." There is no information on the broadside that furnishes the place and precise date of printing—a maddening feature of many broadsides—but for a number of reasons this printing of the address appears to have been nearly contemporaneous with the event itself.

This version of the broadside is the official text of the address as set down in the report of the Pennsylvania Committee at Gettysburg. It varies slightly from the manuscripts in the Library of Congress described as the "first" and "second" drafts. In the broadside the word "power" is not qualified by "poor" and the phrase "under God" toward the end is included. Many Lincoln authorities believe that the latter was interpolated by Lincoln at the moment of delivery, since it does not appear in either of the two earliest surviving drafts in his handwriting, presumably written down before the address was delivered.

When this copy came into the Library's possession as part of the Alfred Whital Stern Collection of Lincolniana, we could trace no other copy, but a year or two later my good friend Thomas W. Streeter wrote to inform me that he had purchased another copy from the Ohio bookseller Ernest Wessen. When I last saw Mr. Wessen in 1961, I asked about the provenance of the Streeter copy, and his only recollection was that it had been kicking around in his attic for a long time. My only consolation lies in the fact that the Streeter copy fetched more at the famous Streeter sale than the purchase price of the copy in the Library of Congress.

Since my retirement nearly two years ago I return to the Library of Congress from time to time, but I hope not too often to become a nuisance to my successor. Last August I had occasion to bring my class of students from the Library School at Catholic University to see at first hand many of the books mentioned in the classroom during the course they had taken under my tutelage. One of the members of the class wanted especially to see the Library's copy of Thucydides' *Opera*, printed by Aldus Manutius at Venice in 1502. I knew the Library had such a copy, but I didn't know this fine example of an Aldine as well perhaps as I should have. When I reexamined it you can imagine my delight at encountering this note in the handwriting of the Rev. Thomas Frognall Dibdin:

A splendid copy of the Editio princeps, very scarce, even in an inferior state. This first Edition of Thucydides is a beautiful book. There are many scholars who prefer the text of this Aldine 2 [sic] that of the greater part of the subsequent Editions. I have known it to produce the sum of 12 pounds 12 shillings. Dibdin

I like to think that my old friend Bill Jackson, who formed a renowned collection of Dibdiniana, would have appreciated this conclusion to this discursive presentation of a few of the pleasures and delights that this erstwhile curator of rare books has encountered in pursuing "The Bibliographical Way."

*One thousand copies designed and
set in type by The Stinehour Press and
printed by The Meriden Gravure Company
on 80-pound Caress Text, Colonial White*